Songbirds

Top Cat

Story by Julia Donaldson

Pictures by Joelle Dreidemy

Series editor Clare Kirtley

OXFORD
UNIVERSITY PRESS

1

Tips for reading Top Cat together

This book practises these sounds:

t p m o c

Ask your child to point to each of these letters and say the sound (e.g. c as in *cat*, not the letter name *cee*). Look out for these letters in the story.

Your child might find this word tricky:

I

Explain that this is a very common word, but you do not sound it out. Say the word for your child if they do not know it.

Before you begin, ask your child to read the title by sounding out and blending. Look at the picture together. What do you think this story is about?

Remind your child to read unfamiliar words by saying the individual sounds and then blending them together quickly to read the word. When you have finished reading the story, look through it again and:

- Talk about the cats' expressions on each page. Ask your child, *How do they feel?*
- Find the words that end with the *p* sound (*top, pop*). Notice that they sound the same at the end of the word. Have fun thinking of some other words that rhyme with *top* and *pop* (*mop, hop, shop, flop, chop, stop*).

I am top cat.

Am I top cat?

I am! I am!

I am top cat.

Am I top cat?

I am! I am!

9

Am I top cat?

Songbirds

Sam's Pot

Story by Julia Donaldson
Pictures by Pauline Siewert
Series editor Clare Kirtley

OXFORD

UNIVERSITY PRESS

11

Tips for reading Sam's Pot together

This book practises these sounds:

s m c t g p a o

Ask your child to point to each of these letters and say the sound (e.g. *m* as in *mum*, not the letter name *em*). Look out for these letters in the story.

Before you begin, ask your child to read the title by sounding out and blending. Look at the picture together. What do you think this story is about?

Remind your child to read unfamiliar words by saying the individual sounds and then blending them together quickly to read the word. When you have finished reading the story, look through it again and:

● Ask your child, *Why did Tom get a mop?* Talk about what Sam is doing on each page.

● Find the words that begin with the *t* sound (*Tom, tap*). Does the *t* sound look the same in all of these words? Talk about capital letters and how they are used for names and at the beginning of sentences. Find some more words that begin with capital letters (*Pam, Sam*). Ask your child, *What sound does the capital letter make in these words?*

Tom got a pot.

Pam got a pot.

Sam got a pot.

Pat, pat, pat!

Tom

A cat

Tap, tap, tap!
Tap, tap, tap!

Tom got a mop!

Songbirds

Bob Bug

Story by Julia Donaldson

Pictures by Deborah Allwright

Series editor Clare Kirtley

OXFORD

UNIVERSITY PRESS

Tips for reading Bob Bug together

This book practises these sounds:

r l d b f h i u s
m c t g p a o

Ask your child to point to each of these letters and say the sound (e.g. *u* as in *umbrella*, not the letter name *yoo*). Look out for these letters in the story.

Before you begin, ask your child to read the title by sounding out and blending. Look at the picture together. What do you think this story is about?

Remind your child to read unfamiliar words by saying the individual sounds and then blending them together quickly to read the word. When you have finished reading the story, look through it again and:

- Ask your child, *Do you think there really was a rat in Bob Bug's bedroom? How do you know?*

- Find the words that begin with the *b* sound (*Bob, Bug, big, bad*). Does the *b* sound look the same in all of these words? Talk about capital letters and how they are used for names and at the beginning of sentences. Find some more words that begin with capital letters (*Mum, Dad*). Ask your child, *What sound does the capital letter make in these words?*

Bob is a bug.

Bob Bug has a mum. His mum
is big.

Bob has a dad. His dad is fit.

Bob has a cup. It has a lid.

Bob has a cot. His cot has a rug.

29

Bob Bug has a hug.

Songbirds

Dig, Dig, Dig!

Story by Julia Donaldson

Pictures by Andy Hammond

Series editor Clare Kirtley

OXFORD
UNIVERSITY PRESS

Tips for reading Dig, Dig, Dig together

This book practises these sounds:

r l d b f h i u s
m t g p a o n

Ask your child to point to each of these letters and say the sound (e.g. *r* as in *rabbit*, not the letter name *ar*). Look out for these letters in the story.

Your child might find this word tricky:

of

Explain that this word is common, but the *f* in *of* is unusual and makes the *v* sound. Say the word for your child if they do not know it.

Before you begin, ask your child to read the title by sounding out and blending. Look at the picture together. What do you think this story is about?

Remind your child to read unfamiliar words by saying the individual sounds and then blending them together quickly to read the word. When you have finished reading the story, look through it again and:

- Talk about Tim and the dog on the last page, are they disappointed? Ask your child, *What did Tim think would be inside the tin?*

- Find the words that begin with the *l* sound (lot, lid, lots). Point to the middle letter in *lid* and ask your child, *What sound does this letter make?* Find more words with the *i* sound in the middle (dig, Tim, his, big). Have fun thinking of some other words with the *i* sound in the middle (wig, him, bin, fit).

Dig, dig, dig!
Tim and his dog had fun.

Dig, dig, dig!
Tim dug up a lot of mud.

Dig, dig, dig!
His dog dug up a rag.

Dig, dig, dig!
Tim dug up a bus.

Dig, dig, dig!
A lid!

Dig, dig, dig!
A big tin!

And in it. . .

lots of bugs!

Songbirds

Zak and the Vet

Story by Julia Donaldson

Pictures by Alan Marks

Series editor Clare Kirtley

OXFORD
UNIVERSITY PRESS

Tips for reading Zak and the Vet together

This book practises these sounds:

v w y z j n k e r d b
f h i u s m c t g a o

Ask your child to point to each of these letters and say the sound
(e.g. *v* as in *van*, not the letter name *vee*). Look out for these letters
in the story.

Your child might find these words tricky:

better he the to will

These words are common, but your child may not have learned how to
sound them out yet. Say the words for your child if they do not know them.

Before you begin, ask your child to read the title by sounding out and
blending. Look at the picture together. What do you think this story
is about?

Remind your child to read unfamiliar words by saying the individual sounds
and then blending them together quickly to read the word. When you have
finished reading the story, look through it again and:

- Ask your child, *Who helped Zak?* Talk about what a vet is.
- Find the words that begin with the *v* sound (*van, vet*). Point to the *e* in
  vet. What sound does this make? Find some other words in the book
  with *e* in the middle (*red, Jen, get, yes*).

Zak did not sit. Zak ran.

Zak ran and ran!

Zak ran in the fog.
A red van hit him.

Jen and Zak went to the vet.

Zak had a bad cut. He had to get a jab.

49

Zak did get better.

wag wag wag

Songbirds

Mum Bug's Bag

Story by Julia Donaldson

Pictures by Deborah Allwright

Series editor Clare Kirtley

OXFORD
UNIVERSITY PRESS

51

Tips for reading Mum Bug's Bag together

This book practises these sounds:

w y z j n k e r d b f
h i u s m c t g p a o

Ask your child to point to each of these letters and say the sound (e.g. *j* as in *jug*, not the letter name *jay*). Look out for these letters in the story.

Your child might find these words tricky:

her of the hole

These words are common, but your child may not have learned how to sound them out yet. Say the words for your child if they do not know them.

Before you begin, ask your child to read the title by sounding out and blending. Look at the picture together. What do you think this story is about?

Remind your child to read unfamiliar words by saying the individual sounds and then blending them together quickly to read the word. When you have finished reading the story, look through it again and:

- Ask your child, *What fell out of Mum Bug's bag?*
- Find the words that end with the *n* sound (*can, pen, fan, bun*). Notice the *u* in *bun*. Find other words in the book with the *u* sound in the middle (*Mum, Yuk, bug*). Have fun thinking of some other words with the *u* sound in the middle (*hum, hug, rug, run*).

Mum Bug has a red bag.
The bag has a zip.

Mum can fit a pen in her bag.

Mum can fit a pen and
a fan in her bag.

Mum can fit a pen and
a fan and
a bun in her bag.

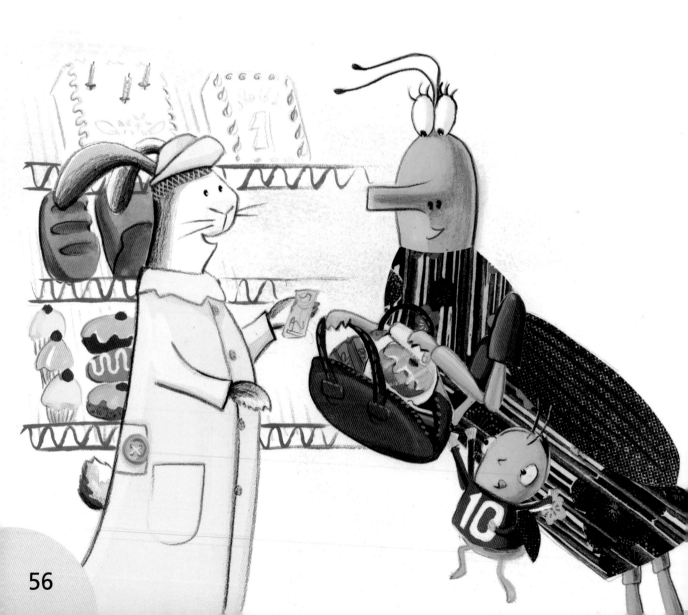

Mum can fit a pen and
a fan and
a bun and
a pot of jam in her bag.

Mum has a hole in her bag!

The pen and
the fan and
the bun and
the jam get wet.

Mum Bug gets a big bag.

Songbirds

Cat Naps

Story by Julia Donaldson

Pictures by Joelle Dreidemy

Series editor Clare Kirtley

OXFORD
UNIVERSITY PRESS

Tips for reading Cat Naps together

This book practises these sounds:

a b c d e g h i k m
n o p r s t u v w y

Ask your child to point to each of these letters and say the sound
(e.g. *b* as in *bug*, not the letter name *bee*). Look out for these
letters in the story.

Your child might find these words tricky:

of and it's

These words are common, but your child may not have learned how to
sound them out yet. Say the words for your child if they do not know them.

Before you begin, ask your child to read the title by sounding out and
blending. Look at the picture together. What do you think this story
is about?

Remind your child to read unfamiliar words by saying the individual sounds
and then blending them together quickly to read the word. When you have
finished reading the story, look through it again and:

* Talk about what Kit Cat might be thinking on page 76.

* Find the words that end with the *p* sound (*top, nap, cap*). Notice that
  cat and *nap* sound the same at the end because they rhyme. Have fun
  thinking of some other words that rhyme with *nap* and *cap* (*tap, map,
  lap, gap*).

Top Cat had a nap in a cap.

Kit Cat had a nap in a sun hat.

Top Cat had a nap in a big top hat.

Kit Cat had a nap on a mat.
Top Cat had a nap on a rug.

Kit Cat had a nap in a cot.
Top Cat had a nap on a bed.

Pad pad pad! Wag wag wag!
Yap yap yap!

It's a dog! Run, Top Cat!
Run, Kit Cat!

Top Cat and Kit Cat had a nap on top of a van.

Songbirds

Pen Fun

Story by Julia Donaldson
Pictures by Judy Brown
Series editor Clare Kirtley

OXFORD
UNIVERSITY PRESS

Tips for reading Pen Fun together

This book practises these sounds:

a b d e f g i j k l m
n o p r s t u v w z

Ask your child to point to each of these letters and say the sound
(e.g. *b* as in *bug*, not the letter name bee). Look out for these letters
in the story.

Your child might find these words tricky:

of gives the to

These words are common, but your child may not have learned how to
sound them out yet. Say the words for your child if they do not know them.

Before you begin, ask your child to read the title by sounding out and
blending. Look at the picture together. What do you think this story
is about?

Remind your child to read unfamiliar words by saying the individual sounds
and then blending them together quickly to read the word. When you have
finished reading the story, look through it again and:

- Ask your child if they think pens are a good present and why.

- Find a word that begins with the *j* sound (*Jez*). Talk about capital letters
  and how they are used for names and at the beginning of sentences.
  Find some more words that begin with capital letters
  (*Rod, Pip, Edwin, Meg, Kev, Dot*). Ask your child, *What sound does
  the capital letter make in these words?*

Rod has a pen.

Pip has a big pen.

Edwin has a big fat pen.

Meg has a big fat red pen.

Kev has a big fat red fun pen.

Dot has a set of big fat red
fun pens.

Jez has ten sets of big fat red fun pens!

Jez gives the pen sets to his pals.

Songbirds

The Big Cod

Story by Julia Donaldson
Pictures by Andy Hammond
Series editor Clare Kirtley

OXFORD
UNIVERSITY PRESS

Tips for reading The Big Cod together

This book practises these sounds:

a b c d e g i m
n o r s t u w y

Ask your child to point to each of these letters and say the sound (e.g. *d* as in *dog*, not the letter name *dee*). Look out for these letters in the story.

Your child might find these words tricky:

the and Tim's

These words are common, but your child may not have learned how to sound them out yet. Say the words for your child if they do not know them.

Before you begin, ask your child to read the title by sounding out and blending. Look at the picture together. What do you think this story is about?

Remind your child to read unfamiliar words by saying the individual sounds and then blending them together quickly to read the word. When you have finished reading the story, look through it again and:

- Talk about if you would rather use a fishing net or a fishing rod and why.

- Find some words in the book that end with the *t* sound (*net, sit, it, bit, wet*). Read each word by sounding out and blending. Which of these words rhyme? Think of other words that rhyme with *net* and *wet* (*bet, get, jet, let, met, pet, set, vet*).

Tim has a net and a can.

Tim's Dad has a rod and a can.

Tim and Dad sit and sit.

87

Dad tugs and tugs.

The cod tugs and tugs.

Dad gets wet.

Songbirds

The Pins and the Pegs

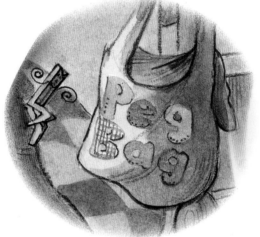

Story by Julia Donaldson
Pictures by Jenny Williams
Series editor Clare Kirtley

OXFORD
UNIVERSITY PRESS

Tips for reading The Pins and the Pegs together

This book practises these sounds:

a b d e f g h j l m
n o p r s t u v

Ask your child to point to each of these letters and say the sound (e.g. *v* as in *van*, not the letter name *vee*). Look out for these letters in the story.

Your child might find these words tricky:

of was the I put let's and

These words are common, but your child may not have learned how to sound them out yet. Say the words for your child if they do not know them.

Before you begin, ask your child to read the title by sounding out and blending. Look at the picture together. What do you think this story is about?

Remind your child to read unfamiliar words by saying the individual sounds and then blending them together quickly to read the word. When you have finished reading the story, look through it again and:

- Talk about why Val was confused (*the pins and the pegs had moved by themselves*).

- Shut the book, then say all the sounds in *bin* separately, and then write the letter that makes each of those sounds. Change one letter to write the word *bun*, then *ban*.

Val had a bag of pegs.

Val had a tin of pins.

Val was in bed.

The pins and the pegs got up.

The pins and the pegs had fun.

97

Val got up.

The pins and the pegs
ran and hid.

Songbirds

Is It?

Story by Julia Donaldson
Pictures by Deborah Allwright, Joelle Dreidemy,
Andy Hammond and Alan Marks
Series editor Clare Kirtley

OXFORD
UNIVERSITY PRESS

Tips for reading Is It? together

This book practises these sounds:

a b c d e f g i j m
n o p r s t u v w y

Ask your child to point to each of these letters and say the sound (e.g. *p* as in *pet*, not the letter name *pee*). Look out for these letters in the story.

Your child might find these words tricky:

what   the   who   bug's   it's   Tim's

These words are common, but your child may not have learned how to sound them out yet. Say the words for your child if they do not know them.

Before you begin, ask your child to read the title by sounding out and blending. Look at the picture together. What do you think this story is about?

Remind your child to read unfamiliar words by saying the individual sounds and then blending them together quickly to read the word. When you have finished reading the story, look through it again and:

- Ask your child, *Where was Top Cat? Why do you think he was hiding there?*

- Read page 99 and find the two words that rhyme (*cat, rat*). Have fun thinking of other words that rhyme with *cat* and *rat* (*mat, hat, bat, sat, pat*). Try to write some of the words. Say all of the sounds in the word separately then write the letter that makes each sound.

What is in Mum Bug's bag?

Is it a wig? Is it a fan? Is it a jug?

Yes, it's a jug!

What is in the fog?

Is it a van? Is it a bus? Is it a jet?

Yes, it's a bus!

Who is in the mud?

Is it Tim? Is it Tim's Dad?
Is it Tim's dog?

Yes, it's Tim!

Who is in bed?

Is it a cat? Is it a dog? Is it a rat?

Yes, it's a cat! It's Top Cat!

Songbirds

Mix, Mix, Mix

Story by Julia Donaldson
Pictures by Deborah Allwright
Series editor Clare Kirtley

OXFORD
UNIVERSITY PRESS

Tips for reading Mix, Mix, Mix together

This book practises these sounds:

> **a b c d e f g i j k l**
> **m n o p r s t u x y**

Ask your child to point to each of these letters and say the sound (e.g. *y* as in *yum*, not the letter name *why*). Look out for these letters in the story.

Your child might find these words tricky:

> **of says and**

These words are common, but your child may not have learned how to sound them out yet. Say the words for your child if they do not know them.

Before you begin, ask your child to read the title by sounding out and blending. Look at the picture together. What do you think this story is about?

Remind your child to read unfamiliar words by saying the individual sounds and then blending them together quickly to read the word. When you have finished reading the story, look through it again and:

- Talk about what Bob Bug's mixture might taste like. Ask your child, *Would you like to eat the mix? Why?*

- Find some words in the book with the *i* sound in them (*big, tins, tips, in, fig, mix, his*). Try to write *tins*. Say all the sounds in the word separately then write the letter that makes each sound.

Bob Bug has a big pan
and a lot of tins.

Bob cuts up a bun.

Bob tips in a pot of jam.

Bob cuts up a lemon, a melon and a fig.

Mix, mix, mix!
Bob rubs his tum.

Bob tips in a lot of nuts.
Mix, mix, mix!

Dad Bug says, "Yuk!"
Mum Bug says, "Yuk!"

But Bob Bug says, "Yum yum!"